Cocktails *for* Drinkers

*Not-Even-Remotely-Artisanal,
Three-Ingredient-or-Less Cocktails that Get to the Point*

JENNIFER McCARTNEY

THE COUNTRYMAN PRESS
A division of W. W. Norton & Company
Independent Publishers Since 1923

For information about permission to reproduce selections from this book, write to
Permissions, The Countryman Press, 500 Fifth Avenue, New York, NY 10110

For information about special discounts for bulk purchases, please contact
W. W. Norton Special Sales at specialsales@wwnorton.com or 800-233-4830

The Countryman Press
www.countrymanpress.com

A division of W. W. Norton & Company, Inc.
500 Fifth Avenue, New York, NY 10110
www.wwnorton.com

Book design by Nick Caruso Design

Library of Congress Cataloging-in-Publication Data
Names: McCartney, Jennifer, 1980– author.
Title: Cocktails for drinkers : not-even-remotely-artisanal, three-ingredient-or-less
cocktails that get to the point / Jennifer McCartney.
Description: Woodstock, VT : Countryman Press,
a division of W. W. Norton & Company, [2016]
"Independent Publishers Since 1923."
Includes index.
Identifiers: LCCN 2015034168
ISBN 978-158157-354-1 (pbk. flexibound)
Subjects: LCSH: Cocktails.
LCGFT: Cookbooks.
Classification: LCC TX951 .P34 2016
DDC 641.87/4—dc23
LC record available at http://lccn.loc.gov/2015034168

10 9 8 7 6 5 4 3 2 1

Table of Contents

Introduction

Real cocktails. Three ingredients or less (plus an optional garnish or two). No artisanal nonsense. No pretentious bartenders wearing suspenders. This book compiles the 100 best cocktails you can make at home with normal ingredients from your fridge or liquor cabinet. For easy reference, the book is organized by type of liquor. Have a bottle of vodka chilling in your freezer? Flip to the vodka section for advice on how to make a summery Greyhound with just grapefruit juice and vodka. Feel like being fancy? Make it a Salty Dog. That's a Greyhound with a salted rim. Sound complicated? I didn't think so. Because of the three-ingredient rule, you won't find classics like the Sazerac, French 75, or Bramble in here, so if you're going to smugly email the publisher about an error, make sure it's related to something besides your missing favorite cocktail—like an actual selling mistake.

And forget about the single serving sizes. These drinks are strong. Make them once and enjoy them for longer, or make two and enjoy them with a friend. Dump in the ingredients and go. No muddling, no shaking— just delicious booze.

Still reading this? Why aren't you drunk yet?

The world has enough artisanal cocktail books. This is a refreshing option for those of us who just want a drink without having to take out a loan, get an anchor tattoo, or grow a hipster beard first. Grab a glass, some ice, some booze, and drink up. I guess you can throw a lime wedge in there if you want, Your Majesty.

Equipment

Here's a secret the fancy bartenders don't want you to know: You don't need equipment to make a cocktail. You don't need a mortar and pestle or a long stainless steel spoon or the mason jar shaker you got for your birthday or a lighter for smoking orange rind. You don't even really need a shot glass for measurement. What's the worst that could happen? Whoops—too much booze in my cocktail! Not a real thing that happens. Use your eyeballs and pour booze from a bottle into a glass filled with ice. Add your second and third ingredients. Stir it. Drink it.

With that said, if you want a cold cocktail but don't want it on the rocks, it's helpful to have a cocktail shaker. Alternately, you can keep all your booze in the freezer.

MY THINKING ON YIELDS: Most of these cocktails have around 4 ounces of liquor and make what I call "a big drink." Cocktails that also require a non-alcoholic mixer like OJ or ginger ale have around 4 ounces of liquor plus a mixer. Those make a large drink or two small drinks because they have more liquid. There are also a bunch of exceptions to this. I probably did the math wrong at some point so if that makes you mad, please email my publisher because they're the ones that made me include measurements in the first place.

A note on the ingredients

Sometimes a recipe may call for a weird thing you don't have. The good news is you can still make the drink without it. Or just move on to a different recipe.

Things you may need:

Bitters

Lime cordial

Grenadine

Simple syrup

These all come premade in bottles and are pretty cheap. Buy a bottle and you'll have it forever. Or just game the system and drink rum and Coke forever.

A note on garnishes

Do you need a lime wedge with your Vodka Cranberry? Nope. Garnishes are pretty much optional. They're there for optics, mainly, so feel free to skip them.

Vodka

The word "vodka" is thought to originate from the
Slavic word "voda," which means "little water." The Russians,
Ukrainians, and Poles have been drinking more than a little
of this liquor as far back as the 8th century, although
its true origins remain murky. Made from distilling grains
like wheat or rye, this liquor is traditionally consumed neat
while wearing a fur hat and arguing about politics.

Vodka Martini

If you've ever worked at a fancy restaurant, you're familiar with the martini-drinker type: Fresh from their yachts and interested to know whether you're serving bay scallops or sea scallops that evening. They always have a vodka preference (Ketel One or Belvedere, usually on the rocks with a twist) and they always tip well. Here's to you, boozy martini-men! Luckily, you don't need an Amex to enjoy this simple cocktail.

Makes one large drink or two small ones

4 ounces vodka
1 ounce dry vermouth
Twist of lemon or a few olives

If you have a cocktail shaker, you can shake the vodka and vermouth around with some ice for an extra-cold beverage. Otherwise, pour the vodka and vermouth into a glass with ice and stir it around. Garnish with a twist of lemon or a few olives.

White Russian

Everyone from Vladimir Putin to your landlady loves these. Whether you're horseback riding shirtless or hanging out on your front stoop slathered in suntan oil while painting your toenails, this is your drink.

Makes one large drink or two small ones

4 ounces vodka
2 ounces Kahlúa
2 ounces light cream

Pour all the ingredients into a glass (literally any glass). Stir with a spoon. Or a fork, we're not fussy. Add some ice cubes. Drink to the Mother Country—whatever yours may be.

"Call me what you like, only give me some vodka."

—*Russian Proverb*

Black Russian

This cocktail was created by a bartender in Brussels in honor of Perle Mesta—the US ambassador to Luxembourg and one of America's most famous socialites at the time. She was on the cover of TIME magazine in 1949 and, in a grand jury testimony after the Watergate scandal, Nixon swore that her diplomatic appointment to Luxembourg had nothing to do with her "big bosoms."

Makes one large drink or two small ones

4 ounces vodka
2 ounces Kahlúa

Combine and serve over ice. Drink to Perle.

Vodka Soda

You don't have to be an aspiring actress living in Los Feliz to enjoy this basically calorie-free cocktail. You can also be working in finance. Either way, this is a strong, straightforward drink that looks good on you, bro.

Makes one large drink or two small ones

4 ounces vodka
8 ounces soda

Pour the ingredients into a glass and stir. Toss in an ice cube and a wedge of lemon. Congratulate yourself on your recent callback/bonus.

Vodka Cranberry

This is like a vodka soda but for women in sororities. It's sweet but strong. Like Blossom-era Joey Lawrence.

Makes one large drink or two small ones

4 ounces vodka
8 ounces cranberry juice
Lime wedge

Mix and serve over ice with a lime wedge.

Vodka Tonic

If you Google "vodka tonic," one of the main search suggestions is "vodka tonic calories." There are 100 calories in a normal vodka tonic. For this recipe, it's more like 200. Just go eat an apple if you're that concerned.

Makes one large drink or two small ones

4 ounces vodka
8 ounces tonic
Lime wedge

Mix and serve over ice. Garnish with a lime wedge.

Greyhound

Everyone knows grapefruit juice is good for you, so start your day off right with this breakfast cocktail of champions.

Makes one large drink or two small ones

4 ounces vodka
8 ounces grapefruit juice

Add the ingredients together and stir. Toss in some ice if you want. Serve with a plate of scrambled eggs or whatever you normally eat for breakfast.

"It was my Uncle George who discovered alcohol was a food well in advance of modern medical thought."

—*P. G. Wodehouse*

Salty Dog

This is a Greyhound with a salted rim. Sound complicated? I didn't think so. Replenish your electrolytes and sodium levels with this even healthier version of a Greyhound. This recipe does get a bit technical as it calls for you to rim your glass with salt. Read on for instructions on the best rimming technique.

Makes one large drink or two small ones

8 ounces grapefruit juice
4 ounces vodka
1 tablespoon rock salt or sea salt

Place salt evenly in a shallow dish. Wet the rim of your glass with water and turn upside down into the salt, ensuring that the rim is covered in salt. Mix the grapefruit juice and vodka and pour into your salt-rimmed glass over ice.

Screwdriver

Next time you open your fridge and see a carton of OJ in the door, just remember that bottle of vodka you have chilling in the freezer. Combine the two for an instant boost of Vitamin C and vodka.

Makes one large drink or two small ones

8 ounces orange juice
4 ounces vodka

Mix the orange juice and vodka together and pour into a glass.

"Once the orange juice wears off, I might be drunk. I love vodka."

—Jarod Kintz

Bloody Mary

Don't let some insufferable twat who writes about mixology for a men's magazine tell you that you can't make a good Bloody Mary with just three ingredients. Sure, you can make it from scratch if you want—Worcestershire sauce, tomato juice, tabasco, salt and pepper, a bunch of olives, a boiled egg—but trust me, if you have a hangover you'll be glad for this simple version with premade mix.

Makes one large drink or two small ones

4 ounces vodka
8 ounces Bloody Mary mix
1 slice of lemon

Pour into a large glass filled with ice and garnish with a lemon slice. Drink to all of last night's bad decisions.

Caesar

Invented in Calgary, Alberta, in 1969 by Italian bartender Walter Chell, the Caesar is essentially a Bloody Mary made with Mott's Clamato juice. While clam juice may sound like an unappetizing thing to add to a cocktail (you're correct), it somehow tastes amazing and Canadians drink upwards of 350 million Caesars a year.

Makes one large drink or two small ones

4 ounces vodka
8 ounces Mott's Clamato juice
4 dashes Worcestershire sauce
1 stalk celery

Mix ingredients and serve over ice. Garnish with the celery. Drink up to seven of these at the Calgary Stampede.

Harvey Wallbanger

Admittedly, this is a somewhat idiotic-sounding thing
to order. Luckily, you can create it at home without having to
make a fool of yourself. This tarted-up Screwdriver made with
Italian liqueur was popular in the 1970s and makes a nice
after-work (or before-work) cocktail.

Makes one large drink or two small ones

4 ounces vodka
8 ounces orange juice
1 ounce Galliano
Slice of orange

Mix the vodka and OJ together and pour over ice. Float the
Galliano on top and add an orange slice, if you'd like.

Moscow Mule

The best Moscow Mule in the world is at The Rarebit in Charleston, South Carolina. Don't even bother making your own. Just get on a plane and go there immediately and give them all your money.

Makes one large drink or two small ones

4 ounces vodka
8 ounces ginger beer
½ ounce lime juice
Slice of lime

Mix the ingredients together and serve over ice. A copper mug isn't necessary, but it keeps your drink colder, longer. So maybe drink all your cocktails out of one of them.

Sea Breeze

The Sea Breeze is a thing thanks to America's cranberry cartels. Big Cranberry just wants you to be full of antioxidants.

Makes one big drink

2 ounces vodka
4 ounces cranberry juice
1 ounce grapefruit juice
Lime wedge

Mix ingredients and serve over ice. Garnish with a lime wedge. If you can arrange to drink this on a yacht in Lake Huron while listening to Jimmy Buffett, that's probably ideal.

Lemon Drop

A Lemon Drop is like licking a cloud or eating part of an angel's wing. Light and airy and a little bit sweet.

Makes one large drink or two small ones

4 ounces vodka
8 ounces lemonade
½ ounce simple syrup
Sugar

Rim a glass with sugar. Pour in the ingredients and stir. Enjoy while cuddling a small kitten or writing a letter to your grandmother.

Fuzzy Navel

It's not 2005 anymore. Body hair is back in a big way.

Makes one large drink or two small ones

4 ounces vodka
2 ounces peach schnapps
8 ounces orange juice

Mix ingredients and rock your fuzzy navel poolside.

Vodka Sprite

This is nothing fancy but it tastes fine. Buy a 20-ounce bottle of Sprite and pour some out. Add the vodka and you have yourself a traveler. Perfect for picnics, subways, and night class.

Makes one large drink or two small ones

4 ounces vodka
8 ounces Sprite

Mix the vodka and Sprite and serve over ice. Or drink it warm because it was in your backpack all day.

Appletini

Hey, congrats! You're old enough to drink!

Makes one large drink

3 ounces vodka
1 ounce apple schnapps

Shake ingredients with ice in a cocktail shaker and serve up.

Espresso Martini

Like Appletinis and Cosmos, this is a martini for people who don't like martinis. You can usually find these at Irish pubs or waterfront patios where the menus list 98 different kinds of martinis. Also available: buffalo chicken sliders, Michelob Ultra, and morning-after regret.

Makes one large drink

2 ounces vodka
1 ounce Kahlúa
1 ounce cold espresso or coffee

Shake ingredients with ice in a cocktail shaker and serve up.

Gin

Ahh, Mother's Ruin. This is the liquor that mothers
in the UK used to give to their infants to keep them
from crying. This is the liquor the Brits rioted over after
the government imposed taxes on it in the 1700s.
This is the liquor my best friend and I stole from her
older brother when we were 14 and then mixed with
Crystal Light lemonade.

Gin and Tonic

This classic British cocktail was originally designed to prevent malaria among soldiers of the British East India Company in India. Now you can drink it to ward off awkward social situations. Also aids in the prevention of memory formation.

Makes one large drink or two small ones

4 ounces gin
8 ounces tonic water
Lime wedge

Mix ingredients together, add lime wedge, and serve over ice.

Gin and Soda

A variation on the vodka soda cocktail, this one offers a bit more bite. Gin basically tastes like pine needles.

Makes one large drink or two small ones

4 ounces gin
8 ounces soda

Mix ingredients together and serve over ice.

"I like to have a martini,
Two at the very most.
After three I'm under
the table, after four I'm
under my host."

—*Dorothy Parker*

Gin Martini

The original, classic cocktail. Served straight up or on the rocks. With a twist or some olives. Shaken or stirred. Martinis are usually made with a brand of Italian vermouth called Martini, which may be where the name came from originally. We'll never know for sure because back then people either wrote stuff down on paper or told their unreliable grandkids instead of blogging about it on the Internet. Thanks to LiveJournal, for example, we know exactly how *House of Leaves* changed your life in 2000.

Makes one large drink

4 ounces gin
1 ounce dry vermouth
Twist of lemon or some olives

Mix the ingredients together and pour over ice for a martini on the rocks. Alternately, mix with ice and then strain into a martini glass to enjoy your cocktail straight up. Garnish with lemon or olives.

Vesper

This is a martini that doubled down. This is what James Bond drinks in Casino Royale. This is vodka, gin, and Lillet Blanc in your mouth at the same time.

Makes one large drink or two small ones

4 ounces gin
2 ounces vodka
1 ounce Lillet Blanc
Twist of lemon

Mix and serve over ice or straight up.

"A perfect martini should be made by filling a glass with gin, then waving it in the general direction of Italy."

—*Noël Coward*

Gin and Juice

If you grew up after the '90s, it may surprise you to know that Snoop Dogg was once kind of a badass. Snoop's classic 1994 song "Gin and Juice" made this drink popular with white suburban kids who sang about how laid-back they were and dreamed of moving to California to surf and smoke weed. Those kids are all accountants now.

Makes one large drink or two small ones

4 ounces gin
8 ounces orange juice

Mix ingredients. Consume while riding shotgun with a shotgun in a lowrider.

Bee's Knees

This cocktail is also an old-timey saying. Isn't it funny how language evolves IRL?

Makes one large drink or two small ones

3 ounces gin
1½ ounces lemon juice
1½ ounces honey

Combine ingredients and serve over ice.

"I try not to drink too much because when I'm drunk, I bite."

—*Bette Midler*

Negroni

This bitter Italian cocktail is as strong as it is delicious. The first time you drink one you instantly become an adult. You basically have to burn all your Ikea furniture immediately and invest in a set of guest towels.

Makes one large drink or two small ones

2 ounces gin
2 ounces Campari
2 ounces sweet vermouth
Orange wheel

Mix the ingredients together and pour over ice. Sorry about your EKTORP sofa, but this cocktail is worth it.

Gimlet

This is the kind of drink you discover in your late twenties. It's more grown-up than a Tom Collins, but not as hard as an actual martini. If this cocktail were a person, it would be a tween.

Makes one large drink

4 ounces gin
2 ounces lime cordial
Lime wedge

Mix and serve straight up or on the rocks. Garnish with the lime.

Gin Buck

This cocktail has nothing to do with deer. The dental formula for deer is:

$$\frac{0.0\text{-}1.3.3}{3.1.3.3}$$

Makes one large drink or two small ones

4 ounces gin
8 ounces ginger beer
½ ounce lemon juice
Lemon wedge

Mix the ingredients and serve over ice with a lemon wedge. What species of deer is your favorite?

"Candy is dandy, but liquor is quicker."

—*Ogden Nash*

Lime Rickey

This is basically a gin and soda but with better marketing. Everyone in *The Great Gatsby* drinks these, for example.

Makes one large drink or two small ones

½ a lime
4 ounces gin
8 ounces soda

Squeeze the lime into a glass filled with ice. Add the gin and soda.

Bloodhound

Bloodhounds were originally bred by monks in 13th-century France. Now they have a cocktail named after them. Finally getting the recognition they deserve.

Makes one large drink

4 strawberries
2 ounces gin
2 ounces sweet vermouth

Mash 3 of the strawberries. Add ice, gin, and vermouth. Garnish with the remaining strawberry.

Gibson

This is a classic martini but with an onion instead of an olive, for some reason. This is Roger Sterling's favorite cocktail on *Mad Men*.

Makes one large drink

4 ounces gin
1 ounce dry vermouth
Silverskin onion

Shake ingredients with ice in a cocktail shaker and serve up. Enjoy your tiny onion.

"When a man who is drinking neat gin starts talking about his mother, he is past all argument."

—*C. S. Forester*

Rum

Most people discover rum cocktails on their first all-inclusive
package vacation to Puerto Vallarta or Ocho Rios.
This liquor, however, could give a shit about your new holiday
bikini. It's too busy telling stories about the good old days
when it was being smuggled by pirates and hidden in caves
and drunk neat by sailors who'd just acquired their first STD.
Remember its outlaw origins while you're drinking your
frozen Bob Marley cocktail and peeing in the pool.

Rum and Coke

You can call it a "Captain and Coke" if you're still in college or you want people to think you're nineteen. My dad drank this a lot when he lived in Kingston, Jamaica, in the '70s. He recommends Appleton Estate rum for the best-tasting cocktail.

Makes one large drink or two small ones

4 ounces dark rum
8 ounces Coke

Mix, pour over ice, and drink on a beach in Negril at sunset to ensure you're making the most of your short life.

Cuba Libre

Cuba is full of Canadian tourists talking about how great it is that there aren't any Americans there. Fun fact: Fidel Castro was once an honorary pallbearer—alongside Jimmy Carter and Leonard Cohen—at the funeral of Canadian Prime Minister, Pierre Trudeau. Anyway. This drink was invented by the Cubans and tastes like revolution.

Makes one large drink or two small ones

4 ounces white rum
8 ounces Coke
Lime wedge

Pour the ingredients over ice, add a squeeze of lime, and toast: *¡Por Cuba libre!* You should know what that means because you probably live in a state that was once part of Mexico. Have some respect for America's native tongue.

Tropical Rum Punch

Rum punch is a party in a bowl. Rum is delicious, pineapple and cranberry juice create a festive pink color, and a bowl of booze at a party signifies that things are going to get sloppy—which puts guests in an optimistic mood. Maybe your coworker's bridal shower will be fun after all!

Makes one party bowl or one really large drink

12 ounces white rum
32 ounces pineapple juice
32 ounces cranberry juice

Pour ingredients into a large bowl filled with ice cubes. Notice how asking your coworker about her wedding colors suddenly seems a lot more bearable.

"Drinking makes uninteresting people matter less, and late at night, matter not at all."

—*Lillian Hellman*

Dark 'n' Stormy

The Dark 'n' Stormy is the national cocktail of Bermuda. This trademarked beverage must be made with Gosling's Black Seal rum (a company founded in Bermuda in 1806) in order to be official. It's long been popular with sailors and other people who like drinking things that taste good.

Makes one large drink or two small ones

4 ounces Gosling's Black Seal rum
8 ounces ginger beer
Lime wedge

Mix the rum and ginger beer together and pour over ice. Serve with a lime wedge.

Spiced Cider

Spiced cider is the perfect fall drink. Consume this from a flask while taking your kids around the neighborhood for Halloween.

Makes one large drink or two small ones

8 ounces warmed apple cider
4 ounces dark rum
Cinnamon

Heat the apple cider and add the rum. Top with a pinch of cinnamon. Drink it quickly because, god, Halloween is super boring when you're not eleven.

Daiquiri

Daiquiris aren't just frozen sugar slushies that come in 48 flavors at your local waterfront dance club. The original daiquiri is a fairly simple recipe that won't give you a massive headache but that also won't lead to a one-night stand. Weigh the pros and cons and decide what's best for you.

Makes one large drink

4 ounces white rum
2 ounces lime juice
1 ounce simple syrup
Sugar

Rim a glass with sugar, add ice, and pour in the rum, lime juice, and simple syrup.

Macuá

This became the national drink of Nicaragua in 2006 after a competition sponsored by a local rum company. The winning recipe was created by a pediatrician from Granada who named the drink after a tropical bird.

Makes one large drink or two small ones

4 ounces white rum
4 ounces guava juice
2 ounces lemon juice
Lemon wedge

Mix ingredients and serve over ice with a lemon wedge.

"I feel sorry for people who don't drink. When they wake up in the morning, that's as good as they're going to feel all day."

—*Dean Martin*

Whiskey, Bourbon, and Rye

Look, I know I said there were no rules, but this is
just common sense: single-malt whisky is for drinking straight
or with a splash of water. For these recipes, use a
blended Scottish whisky, Irish whiskey, American bourbon,
or Canadian rye.

Jack and Coke

This is a fairly standard cocktail that people like to order because it shows they know what brand of liquor they want in their drink. If you order a "whiskey and Coke" or "bourbon and Coke," you're demonstrating to the bartender that you've heard of alcohol but don't know enough about it to be specific.

Makes one large drink or two small ones

4 ounces Jack Daniels (or other bourbon)
8 ounces Coke

Mix the bourbon and Coke and pour over ice.

Jack and Diet

People go nuts for the taste of Diet Coke, regardless of whether they're actually on a diet.

Makes one large drink or two small ones

4 ounces Jack Daniels (or other bourbon)
8 ounces Diet Coke

Mix the bourbon and Diet Coke and pour over ice. Thank Rumsfeld for making your aspartame headache possible.

Rye and Ginger

A Rye and Ginger is a classic Canadian cocktail. I attended the University of Guelph with an aggie who would drink a mickey's worth of these before heading out to the Bullring.*

Makes one large drink or two small ones

4 ounces rye
8 ounces ginger ale
Lime wedge

Combine ingredients, add a lime wedge, and serve over ice.

* *See a Canadian dictionary (Southeastern Ontario dialect) for American translation.*

Whiskey Soda

This is a great-tasting drink. You get great whiskey flavor without the on-your-ass strength of straight whiskey, which means you can drink this all night without worrying about getting so drunk that you punch a wall or destroy a friend of a friend's not-quite-yet-installed granite kitchen countertop by leaning on it even though there's a sign like DO NOT LEAN. The soda is also sort of good for you.

Makes one large drink or two small ones

4 ounces whiskey
8 ounces soda

Mix together and pour over ice. Drink until you get nostalgic about your life-changing trip to Scotland or Ireland when you were twenty-two, or until you're asked to leave the house party.

Whiskey Sour

This is another classic that's fallen out of style. Sours are a nice option if you like a softer-tasting cocktail without the hard edge of straight booze.

Makes one large drink

3 ounces rye
1½ ounces lemon juice
1 ounce simple syrup

Combine ingredients and serve over ice.

Manhattan

The word Manhattan is from the Lenape "Manna-hata" which means "land of many hills." The more you know.

Makes one large drink or two small ones

2 ounces rye
1 ounce sweet vermouth
Dash of bitters

Combine and serve up or on the rocks.

Rob Roy

Similar to the Manhattan, this cocktail is made exclusively with whiskey rather than rye. Named after the 1894 operetta Rob Roy, which the *New York Times* called "clean, frank, manly, bright, and winsome," this cocktail lives up to its fancy origins. Probably.

Makes one large drink

2 ounces whiskey
1 ounce sweet vermouth
Dash of bitters

Combine and serve up or on the rocks.

"There is no bad whiskey. There are only some whiskeys that aren't as good as others."

—*Raymond Chandler*

Old Fashioned

I have a friend who brings her own Old Fashioned ingredients to house parties, including the orange. This is a delicate maneuver to pull off without seeming insane, but it is super endearing. May you always pursue drunkenness via your favorite cocktail with this level of determination (without being a dick about it).

Makes one large drink

Dash of bitters
1 teaspoon sugar
3 ounces bourbon
Orange twist

Add bitters to sugar until sugar has had enough. Add ice and bourbon and stir. Garnish with an orange twist.

"Alcohol, taken in sufficient quantities, may produce all the effects of drunkenness."

—*Oscar Wilde*

Hot Toddy

People in Scotland don't go to hospitals. They just drink these and feel better.

Makes one large drink because you want to get better quickly

4 ounces boiling water
2 ounces blended whisky
1 tablespoon honey

Pour boiling water over the whisky and honey in a heat-safe mug. Go read *Lanark* by Alasdair Gray.

Boulevardier

A Boulevardier is like a Negroni but with bourbon instead of gin. *The New York Times Style Magazine* calls this "a marvel of a cocktail with an enviably colorful peerage."

Makes one large drink or two small ones

2 ounces bourbon
2 ounces sweet vermouth
2 ounces Campari
Orange peel

Combine ingredients and serve over ice with a bit of orange peel. Marvel with your friends about its colorful peerage.

Seven and Seven

I worked at a place where a server once brought a man a Seagram's 7 neat at seven o'clock because she thought he said "a Seagram's 7 at seven."

Makes one large drink or two small ones

4 ounces Seagram's 7
8 ounces 7Up

Mix and serve over ice at any time you want.

**"I went out with a guy who once told me
I didn't need to drink to make myself more fun to
be around. I told him, I'm drinking so that
you're more fun to be around."**

—*Chelsea Handler*

Bourbon Peach Sweet Tea

Go find yourself a porch and drink one of these on it.

Makes one large drink or two small ones

4 ounces bourbon
8 ounces sweetened peach tea

Mix the ingredients and serve over ice.

All American

What's more American than bourbon, SoCo, and Coke? Maybe Bruce Springsteen or those inflatable pumpkin lawn ornaments everyone buys at Halloween.

Makes one large drink or two small ones

2 ounces bourbon
2 ounces Southern Comfort
4 ounces Coke

Combine ingredients and serve over ice.

Mint Julep

You have to mention the Kentucky Derby when you talk about Mint Juleps. Horses love these.

Makes one large drink or two small ones

4 mint leaves
4 ounces bourbon
2 teaspoons simple syrup
Sprig of mint

Mash the mint leaves using your marbled mortar and pestle from Williams-Sonoma. Or tear the leaves with your hands. Add the bourbon and simple syrup, adorn with a sprig of mint, and serve to your Thoroughbred over crushed ice.

Revolver

The Revolver was invented by California bartender, Jon Santer. It's nice to drink in winter and is also what German shepherds should carry in their flasks when they come to rescue you.

Makes one large drink or two small ones

2 ounces bourbon
1 ounce Kahlúa
Dash of bitters
Orange peel

Mix ingredients in a cocktail shaker and serve chilled with an orange peel.

"First you take a drink, then the drink takes a drink, then the drink takes you."

—F. Scott Fitzgerald

Rusty Nail

Everyone knows that when you go real camping (not RV camping), you can't bring beer. It's heavy and your fellow campers will kill you if you make them portage a backpack that has beer weighing it down. That's why you bring a flask of something strong instead.

Makes one large drink

3 ounces whiskey
1½ ounces Drambuie

Mix the whiskey and Drambuie and drink until you forget about the black flies.

Eggnog

Eggnog is an acquired taste (an acquired bad taste) but if you're into warm milk, this is the cocktail for you. Everyone talks this up at Christmas and says things like, "First eggnog of the year!"—but I guarantee you can only drink one of these before switching to something that isn't warm milk.

Makes one large drink or two small ones

4 ounces bourbon
3 tablespoons eggnog mix
8 ounces milk, warmed
Garnish with nutmeg

Mix the ingredients together and top with grated nutmeg. Or, honestly, just drink a beer.

Tequila

In university, everyone on our floor chipped in for
as many bottles of tequila as we could afford. We had
a tequila party and one guy had to be taken
away on a gurney by the paramedics. The lesson here
is don't let your kids go to college.

Paloma

Straight tequila is great for those evenings you don't want to remember. But some of us like a sophisticated tequila cocktail. One made with soda pop. Drink up, fancy-pants. You're basically Kate Middleton.

Makes one large drink or two small drinks

2 ounces tequila
6 ounces Fresca (or any grapefruit-flavored soda)
Lime wedge

Pour the ingredients into a glass. Stir them up. Add a lime wedge and some ice cubes and serve. Repeat until you start arguing about religion with your dinner guests.

"One tequila, two tequila, three tequila, floor."

—*George Carlin*

Tequila Sunrise

This drink was supposedly popularized by Mick Jagger in the 1970s. And who am I to argue with Wikipedia?

Makes one large drink or two small ones

4 ounces tequila
8 ounces orange juice
1 ounce grenadine

Mix the tequila and OJ and pour over ice. Top with the grenadine. People in the know say it looks like a sunrise.

Matador

On *Bullfighting* by A. L. Kennedy is a very good book about bullfighting. Sorry, Hemingway. Read it while drinking a Matador—the margarita's lesser-known cousin made with pineapple juice.

Makes one large drink

3½ ounces tequila
2 ounces pineapple juice
1½ ounces lime cordial

Combine ingredients and serve over ice.

"O tequila, savage water of sorcery, what confusion and mischief your sly, rebellious drops do generate!"

— *Tom Robbins*

"It's 4:58 on Friday afternoon. Do you know where your margarita is?"

—*Amy Neftzger*

Margarita

Margaritas taste like a vacation. Drink one for lunch at your cubicle with your sad desk salad and see how much better you feel.

Makes one large drink

3½ ounces tequila
2 ounces Cointreau
1½ ounces lime cordial
Lime wedge

Combine and serve over ice with a lime.

Brandy

Brandy is made by distilling wine. It's kind of sweet
and generally considered an after-dinner drink.
Cognac is probably the most popular variety, with brands
like Courvoisier, Hennessy, and Rémy Martin.
Drink this and become rich or vice versa.

Sidecar

Sidecars were named for those little one-seater motorcycle attachments popular both in real life and in Indiana Jones movies. Why not just sit behind the driver? Regardless of how you get around, as long as you're not driving you can enjoy one of these.

Makes one large drink or two small ones

4 ounces Cognac
2 ounces Cointreau
2 ounces lemon juice

Combine and drink in a bar in Paris to toast the end of the Great War.

"A lady came up to me one day and said 'Sir! You are drunk,' to which I replied 'I am drunk today madam, and tomorrow I shall be sober but you will still be ugly.'"

—*Winston S. Churchill*

Brandy Milk Punch

My mom used to give me warm milk to help me fall asleep when I was younger. I found out years later she also spiked it with brandy. This was back when moms did stuff like that and drank Guinness when they were pregnant and society wasn't so uptight.

Makes one large drink or two small ones

3 ounces Cognac
2 ounces simple syrup
2 ounces half and half
Pinch of nutmeg

Combine ingredients and serve over ice. Top with nutmeg if you own more spices than salt and pepper.

Stinger

This is an old school after-dinner drink. You may have a great-uncle who still drinks these.

Makes one large drink

3 ounces brandy
1 ounce crème de menthe

Mix the ingredients and sip slowly after dinner.

Between the Sheets

This saucy 1920s cocktail hearkens back to an age when drinks had sexy names.

Makes one large drink or two small ones

1½ ounces brandy
1½ ounces Cointreau
1½ ounces gin

Combine with ice in a cocktail shaker and serve up.

Brandy Alexander

This sweet-tasting cocktail is basically a milkshake. It was created during Prohibition to mask poor-quality hooch. Alcohol is legal again, so that's probably why this drink has fallen out of fashion.

Makes one large drink or two small ones

2 ounces Cognac
2 ounces white crème de cacao
2 ounces light cream

Combine ingredients, ideally in a cocktail shaker with ice. Serve straight up.

Horse's Neck

Haha. Wut. Horse's Neck.

Makes one large drink or two small ones

4 ounces Cognac
8 ounces ginger beer
Dash of bitters
Lemon twist

Combine and serve over ice. Pretend the lemon twist is the neck of a horse.

Cognac Sparkler

Hard apple cider is making a comeback. It used to be that if you wanted real cider, you had to travel to southwest England, where all the cider is basically rubbing alcohol and drinking half a mug gives you hallucinations. But thanks to all the hipster apples in the Pacific Northwest, you can now get your hands on good US cider pretty much anywhere. If you can't get enough booze in your booze, try adding Cognac and a dash of bitters.

Makes one large drink

1 ounce Cognac
1 bottle hard apple cider
Dash of bitters

Pour the cognac into a glass and top with the hard apple cider and dash of bitters.

Champagne and Prosecco

Bubbly, bubbly, bubbly! Champagne is from France.
Prosecco is from Italy. These are drinks for celebrations like
divorce parties or your cross-country Amtrak journey.

Mimosa

The drink that's graced thousands of brunches, bridal showers, weddings, baby showers, and early-morning breast-feeding sessions. Basically, this sweet nectar is for getting your day-drunk on while allowing you to feel slightly sophisticated because: champagne!

Makes a bunch of drinks since, once you open a bottle of champagne, you've committed

1 bottle champagne
1 container no-pulp orange juice

Pour equal parts champagne and orange juice into a glass. Toast to something good, like your UTI that's recently cleared up.

Kir Royale

People love to order these, if only to smugly explain to their friends that a Kir Royale is made with crème de cassis, which is a blackcurrant liqueur, and which they discovered on a backpacking trip to France where they stayed with their dad's old business partner who lived with his second wife in a restored farmhouse in Provence and who drank a lot even by French standards.

Makes a bunch of drinks

1 bottle champagne
1 bottle crème de cassis

Fill a glass with champagne two-thirds full and add a half-ounce of crème de cassis. The purple liqueur will slowly sink to the bottom and look pretty, if that's important to you.

"There comes a time in every woman's life when the only thing that helps is a glass of champagne."

—*Bette Davis*

St-Germain and Champagne

St-Germain is a light-tasting liqueur made from elderflowers. Champagne is made from grapes, probably. Combine the two and you've got a lovely, light cocktail for drinking in your garden.

Makes one glass

1 glass champagne
½ ounce St-Germain

Pour a glass full of champagne and top with a half-ounce of St-Germain.

Bellini

The Bellini was invented at the famous Harry's Bar in Venice, a spot frequented by Ernest Hemingway and Orson Welles. It's also the kind of cocktail moms order when they're out for a family dinner at a chain restaurant. You can make this with champagne instead of prosecco, but don't tell Italy.

Makes a bunch of cocktails

1 bottle prosecco
1 bottle white peach juice

Pour one part prosecco and two parts peach juice into a glass. Toast to your kid's high school graduation. And can we get some more bread over here?

Sparkling Grapefruit Cocktail

This recipe calls for both grapefruit bitters and Lillet Rosé, which you probably don't have. If you do, go for it. Here's the recipe.

Makes one large cocktail

4 ounces champagne
2 ounces Lillet Rosé
4 dashes grapefruit bitters

Combine and serve at your Super Bowl party.

Aperol Spritz

Aperol is an herbal liqueur that tastes like your first day in Rome when the sun comes out and you've just ordered a pastry in Italian and you're sitting next to a fountain built hundreds of years ago and you really feel alive for the first time in your life. Mix it with prosecco and club soda, but if you're traveling there in 2004 don't buy any CDs purporting to be Britney's Greatest Hits. It's definitely just Italian opera music.

Makes one large drink or two small ones

6 ounces prosecco
4 ounces Aperol
2 ounces club soda
Lemon twist

Mix the ingredients in a glass and add an ice cube or two. Top with a lemon twist.

Hummingbird

The Hummingbird has a great name and it's a light cocktail perfect for day-drinking. Actual hummingbirds are amazing and worth reading up on. The Aztec god of war was depicted as a hummingbird, for example.

Makes one large drink or two small ones

4 ounces champagne
3 ounces St-Germain
4 ounces club soda
Lemon wedge

Mix, garnish, and drink to all the tiny, beautiful animals in the world.

"Champagne is appropriate for breakfast, lunch, or dinner."

—Madeline Puckette

Wine

There's a lot you could know about wine.
The main thing is not to feel intimidated by all that you
definitely don't know. Buy a bottle based on the label
like 98% of the world does and enjoy mixing it with
Coke or club soda.

White Wine

Wine is made from grapes and comes in a bottle or a box. There's just the one ingredient so it's a great recipe to practice with.

Makes one large drink

1 bottle white wine

Open the wine and let it breathe. Just kidding. Pour it in a large glass immediately and drink it up like a suburban housewife.

"**What wine goes with Captain Crunch?**"

—*George Carlin*

Red Wine

Once you've mastered white wine you can branch out to various different kinds of wine. This red wine is made with red wine.

Makes one large drink

1 bottle red wine

You know what to do.

Kir

If you're down to your last bottle of white wine that you got for free at a PR event promoting Florida vineyards—this is the cocktail for you. Take your shitty wine and add some crème de cassis. Now you have a delicious cocktail. Thanks, France!

Makes a bunch of drinks

1 bottle crème de cassis
1 bottle white wine

Add a half-ounce of the crème de cassis to a full glass of wine. Continue until the bottle is gone.

Wine Spritzer

Adding seltzer water to sauv blanc is the preferred way to consume your morning wine on the Upper East Side. If you love a bit of alcohol early in the morning, or early afternoon, or late evening, this is the drink for you.

Makes a bunch of drinks

1 bottle club soda
1 bottle white wine

Add a splash of soda to a full glass of wine. Take your horse to the vet. Dust your money piles.

Tinto de Verano

If you like pouring soda pop into your wine, then you'll love this. Luckily, the Italian name keeps it from sounding like something a sixteen-year-old would drink at a house party before throwing up in the bushes outside.

Makes one large drink

4 ounces red wine
4 ounces Sprite
Lemon wedge

Combine and serve on the rocks. Top with a lemon wedge.

Cooler by the Lake

Don't drink this out of a pink plastic tumbler on a beach in New Jersey. You're not fooling anyone and the beach police will give you a ticket for drinking in public. Save it for drinking by actual lakes where the resources of our police state are stretched thinner. Get yourself a cabin, a hammock, a Janet Evanovich novel, and enjoy.

Makes one large drink

4 ounces white wine
2 ounces peach schnapps
6 ounces cranberry juice
Lime wedge

Combine ingredients over ice, add a lime wedge, and drink until the sun sets.

Kalimotxo

This is a cocktail popular in the Basque regions of France and Spain. Fun fact: The Basques were some of the earliest inhabitants of Western Europe, and their society was matrilineal.

Makes one large drink or two small ones

4 ounces red wine
4 ounces Coke

Combine and serve over ice.

"And in my mind, this settles the issue. I would never drink cologne, and am therefore not an alcoholic."

—*Augusten Burroughs*

Beer

Still drinking your beer straight? Get with the program.
These are cocktails you can make by adding stuff to beer.

Classic Shandy

A shandy is for those occasions when you feel the need to water down your beer. While traditionally made with lemonade, you can also use lemon-lime soda or whatever else floats your boat.

Makes one large drink

4 ounces beer
4 ounces lemonade

Mix the beer and lemonade.

Grapefruit Shandy

This is a refreshing cocktail because grapefruit juice is amazing and you can pair it with anything. Lamb curry? Add a cup of grapefruit juice. Chicken parm? Grapefruit. Birthday cake? Grapefruit.

Makes one large drink or two small ones

4 ounces beer
4 ounces grapefruit juice

Mix the ingredients and enjoy the best the citrus family has to offer.

Boilermaker

A boilermaker is for those occasions when a beer isn't going to cut it but doing a shot feels a bit dramatic.

For example, this is fun to order if you're back in the Midwest for an aunt's funeral and also wearing a Toledo Mud Hens baseball hat that you've owned since high school. Or also, if you're in a hipster bar in Brooklyn that's designed to look like a bar in the Midwest. That's fine too.

Makes one large drink

Shot of whiskey
Glass of beer

Drop the whiskey into the beer and drink the mixture quickly. Repeat until you forget the names of all the Great Lakes.

"Beer . . . now there's a temporary solution."

—*Homer Simpson*

Michelada

There are many ways to make a Michelada, but basically it's beer with tomato juice and hot sauce. This tastes best with light beer like Dos Equis or Duff.

Makes one large drink

1 bottle beer
2 ounces tomato juice
½ ounce hot sauce
Lime wedge

Mix the ingredients and serve over ice with a lime wedge.

Guinness Milkshake

If you're one of those people who are constantly like, Why can't my cocktails be more like my eighth birthday party? . . . you're in luck. This beer milkshake is all of the childhood and none of the sophistication.

Makes one large milkshake or two small ones

2 scoops vanilla ice cream
1 can Guinness

Scoop the ice cream into a glass and top with Guinness. Remind your friends about the time you visited the Guinness brewery in Dublin.

Campari & IPA

This cocktail is just liqueur added to beer, you're thinking. You're right. But guess what? It tastes nice. IPA is hoppy and Campari is bitter and together they make this a great option for when you've run out of everything and are like, what can I make with this leftover can of Lagunitas and a half-full bottle of Campari?

Makes one large drink

6 ounces IPA
2 ounces Campari

Combine beer and liqueur and serve over ice.

Snakebite

This beer cocktail is popular in the UK. Bill Clinton once ordered it in England and the bartender refused to make it for him.

Makes one large drink

1 can beer
1 bottle hard cider

Mix equal parts beer and cider in a glass.

Assorted Liquors and Liqueurs

This section makes use of those random bottles in your liquor cabinet.

Amaretto and Coke

This is a very sweet cocktail that tastes like slightly medicinal Coca-Cola. You probably shouldn't drink this after the age of fifteen because you can afford to buy real booze now and not steal it from your parent's liquor cabinet before heading out to a party in a vacant field the next town over. Those were good parties. When you're older, parties become "dinner parties" and are basically just your married friends exchanging kitchen contractor stories and then rushing home to relieve the babysitter at eleven.

Makes one large drink or two small ones

2 ounces amaretto
6 ounces Coke
Lime wedge

Mix the ingredients together and pour into a glass with ice. Garnish with a lime if you don't want scurvy.

"I know a man who gave up smoking, drinking, sex, and rich food. He was healthy right up to the day he killed himself."

—*Johnny Carson*

Sweet South

If you've often complained that peach schnapps is just not sweet enough for you, don't worry. On a sweetness scale of one to Ariana Grande, this is an eleven.

Makes one large drink or two small ones

4 ounces peach schnapps
8 ounces Mountain Dew

Mix the ingredients together and serve over ice. Congratulations! You now have eight cavities.

Venetian Cup

This is the kind of drink you'll be served at a rustic summer barn wedding where the paper lanterns are plentiful and the guests are all social media strategists. The drink will be served in a repurposed soda bottle and come with one of those red and white paper straws. Cheers to Savannah and Elliot for allowing us all to get drunk on such a trendy, delicious cocktail.

Makes one large drink or two small ones

2 ounces Campari
1 ounce Pimm's No. 1
6 ounces ginger beer

Combine Campari and Pimm's over ice. Add the ginger beer.

Redheaded Ginger

While the name is redundant, you can still enjoy this cocktail made with Lillet Rouge and ginger beer.

Makes one large drink or two small ones

4 ounces Lillet Rouge
8 ounces ginger beer

Combine and toast to Ron Weasley and redheaded gingers everywhere.

**"When I read about the evils of drinking,
I gave up reading."**

—*Henny Youngman*

Pimm's No. 1 Cup

This is so British it's basically a walk on the moors, a browse through the Daily Mail, a pint of cider in Somerset, a bank holiday, an opinion about Princess Charlotte's christening dress, and Katie Price all rolled into one cocktail. I drank this at a "knees-up" celebrating the marriage of Prince William and Kate in Knightsbridge.

Makes one large drink or two small ones

1 bottle Pimm's No. 1

Drink this neat, on the rocks, or mixed with lemonade or club soda.

Caipirinha

Brazil's national cocktail is made with Cachaça, which is a liquor similar to rum. They take it pretty seriously because this exists: The Brazilian Institute of Cachaça. The liquor is strong, so don't embarrass yourself.

Makes one large drink

4 lime wedges
2 teaspoons sugar
5 ounces Cachaça
Lime wedge

Mash the limes and sugar together in a glass until well smushed. Add some ice and pour in the Cachaça. Garnish with the final lime wedge.

Southern Belle

Southern Comfort was first invented and bottled by a bartender from New Orleans in the 1800s. One of the original slogans was "Two per customer. No gentleman would ask for more." You probably don't need more than two bottles of Southern Comfort around anyway, unless you're a prepper.

Makes one large drink or two small ones

4 ounces Southern Comfort
8 ounces root beer

Mix the two ingredients and serve over ice. Or save the unopened bottles in your underground bunker for when Operation Jade Helm becomes a reality.

Americano

This Italian cocktail got its start in the 1860s and was supposedly invented by the same guy who invented Campari. Americans loved it. Hence the name.

Makes one large drink or two small ones

2 ounces Campari
2 ounces sweet vermouth
Splash of club soda

Combine and serve over ice.

Irish Float

Baileys just tastes good. Drinking it gives you the same calm feeling you get from petting a long-haired cat or clearing out your email inbox. Adding Coke intensifies that feeling.

Makes one large drink

4 ounces Baileys Irish Cream
4 ounces Coke

Combine and serve over ice.

Brown Cow

How now, brown cow?

Makes one large drink

4 ounces Kahlúa
8 ounces milk
Nutmeg

Combine and serve over ice. Sprinkle with nutmeg.

Stars and Stripes

Patriotism takes many forms, so why not display yours via this very American sugar cocktail. Look, this obviously doesn't taste all that great but it looks cool and is fun to serve at parties.

Makes one cocktail

2 ounces grenadine
2 ounces heavy cream
2 ounces blue curaçao

Pour each ingredient slowly into a glass in the order given above, being careful not to let them mix. Garnish with some American exceptionalism.

Acknowledgments

Thanks to my editor, Ann Treistman, and to Sarah Bennett at The Countryman Press. Thanks to everyone in marketing, sales, and publicity at W. W. Norton. Thanks, booze.

Index

31901059495079